D0385095

Buddhism for Sheep

Buddhism for Sheep

Illustrated by Chris Riddell

Text by Louise Howard

St. Martin's Press
New York

BUDDHISM FOR SHEEP. Copyright © 1996 by Chris Riddell and Louise Howard.
All rights reserved. Printed in the United States of America. No part of this
book may be used or reproduced in any manner whatsoever without written
permission except in the case of brief quotations embodied in critical articles
or reviews. For information, address St. Martin's Press, 175 Fifth Avenue,
New York, N.Y. 10010.

Designed by Martin Lovelock

Library of Congress Cataloging-in-Publication Data

Riddell, Chris.
        Buddhism for sheep / illustrated by Chris Riddell ; text by Louise
Howard.
              p.   cm.
        ISBN 0-312-14556-X
        1. Buddhism—Caricatures and cartoons.   2. Buddhism—Humor.
I. Howard, Louise.   II. Title.
BQ4060.R53   1996
294.3'0207—dc20   96-25622
                                                         CIP

First published in Great Britain in 1996 by Ebury Press

10   9   8   7   6   5

contents

Living

There are two ways of looking—a right way . . .

. . . and a wrong way

Pay attention to the bodily processes

Every second of life is a miracle

Life is everchanging

Live in the present, . . .

. . . not the future

The stinking pen and the fragrant rose
are two aspects of the same existence

Do not consider your possessions to be yours alone

Respect all living beings . . .

. . . and inanimate objects

Consider the impurities of your body

Every article entrusted to you must
be used with good care

Travel alone rather than with a fool

Make time simply to stop and listen

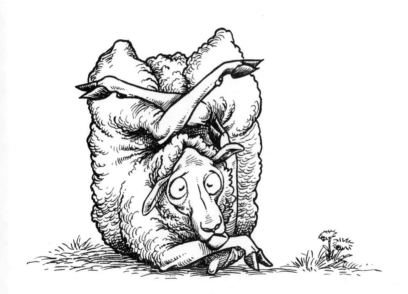

Good posture is essential for meditation

Cultivate the path to liberation; the ultimate
liberation lies beyond the horizon of daily life

Foolish
Thinking

WOLF!

Do not spread news if you
are uncertain of its truth

Do not hoard possessions for their own sake

Misfortune accompanies fortune

Infatuation may block spiritual progress

The demon of worldly desire
is always seeking chances to
deceive the mind

The foolish are unaware of their mistakes

Confidence must be balanced with wisdom

Misled by error you may become a demon

It is our own anger that destroys us

Remember that it is easy to point out the mistakes
of others but difficult to admit one's own

Not by enmity are enmities overcome

Beware the evil or insincere friend;
he is more to be feared than a wild beast

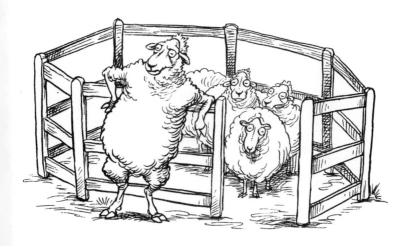

Do not rely upon the industry of others

Enlightenment

Do not seek to avoid or postpone your present duty

Be careful of your first steps into anything

Don't forget what you are seeking

The road to the experience of ultimate reality
is the practice of meditation

If you master the situation you are in you can
no longer be driven around by circumstances

Persevere, even in the face of repeated failure

There is a deep serenity in distancing
oneself from all life processes

Do not let your mind be disturbed, . . .

. . . even in the most difficult circumstances

Train your mind; it is the source of everything

Those who do not follow the true path to
enlightenment may experience mental delusions

Accept the challenge
of higher development

Rely upon yourself; do not
depend upon anyone else

Reality

Karma means there is no escape

The body may waste away but the mind
becomes more and more settled

It is necessary to gain the insight
that life is impermanent

With a clear gaze reflect serenely on reality

We are wrong if we think there is time . . .

Life is nothing but suffering and pain

Those who act well and have good karma
will be reborn into happiness . . .